NEVERMORE

THE RAVEN

NEVERMORE

A Photobiography of Edgar Allan Poe

KAREN E. LANGE

OTHER POEMS

NATIONAL GEOGRAPHIC

WASHINGTON, D.C.

BY

To my mother, who taught me to love books, and my father, who taught me to love stories.

PUBLISHED BY THE NATIONAL GEOGRAPHIC SOCIETY
John M. Fahey, Jr., *President and Chief Executive Officer*
Gilbert M. Grosvenor, *Chairman of the Board*
Tim T. Kelly, *President, Global Media Group*
John Q. Griffin, *President, Publishing*
Nina D. Hoffman, *Executive Vice President; President, Book Publishing Group*

PREPARED BY THE BOOK DIVISION
Nancy Laties Feresten, *Vice President, Editor in Chief, Children's Books*
Bea Jackson, *Director of Design and Illustrations, Children's Books*
Amy Shields, *Executive Editor, Series, Children's Books*
Jennifer Emmett, *Executive Editor, Reference and Solo, Children's Books*
Carl Mehler, *Director of Maps*

STAFF FOR THIS BOOK
Virginia Koeth, *Editor*
Lori Epstein, Charlotte Fullerton, *Illustrations Editors*
Marty Ittner, *Designer*
Matt Chwastyk, *Map Production*
Connie B. Binder, *Indexer*
Lewis Bassford, *Production Project Manager*
Jennifer A. Thornton, *Managing Editor*
Grace Hill, *Associate Managing Editor*
R. Gary Colbert, *Production Director*
Susan Borke, *Legal and Business Affairs*

MANUFACTURING AND QUALITY MANAGEMENT
Christopher A. Liedel, *Chief Financial Officer*
Phillip L. Schlosser, *Vice President*
Chris Brown, *Technical Director*
Nicole Elliott, *Manager*

The body text of the book is set in Minion Pro.
The display text is Archive Autograph Script and Numbskull.

Printed in the United States of America

LIBRARY OF CONGRESS CATALOGING-IN-PUBLICATION DATA
Lange, Karen E.
  Nevermore : a photobiography of Edgar Allan Poe / by Karen Lange.
    p. cm.
  Includes bibliographical references and index.
  ISBN 978-1-4263-0398-2 (hardcover : alk. paper)—ISBN 978-1-4263-0399-9 (lib. bdg. : alk. paper)
  1. Poe, Edgar Allan, 1809-1849—Juvenile literature. 2. Poe, Edgar Allan, 1809-1849—Pictorial works—Juvenile literature. 3. Authors, American—19th century—Biography—Juvenile literature. I. Title.
  PS2631.L25 2009   818'.309—dc22
  [B]   2008039833

COVER: Poe in November 1848, less than a year before he died. He was at his saddest and most sickly, suffering from the effects of a suicide attempt and heavy drinking. Sarah Helen Whitman, whom Poe was courting, thought the photo captured the writer's journey to the "Ultima Thule"—Greek for "the limits of discovery." In Poe's words: "a wild weird clime, that lieth, sublime, Out of SPACE—out of TIME."

HALF TITLE: An ominous bird drawn by Edouard Manet illustrates an 1875 French edition of Poe's most famous poem, "The Raven." Within a generation of his death, Poe's works and life were inspiring writers and artists in France and across Europe.

TITLE PAGE: An engraving of Poe, based on a photo, decorates the opening page of a volume of his poetry.

OPPOSITE: Somber and still for the camera, Poe posed for this early photo, called a daguerreotype, in May or June of 1849. He was visiting Annie L. Richmond, whose companionship he sought after his wife Virginia died.

ACKNOWLEDGMENTS: Thank you to Chris Semtner, curator of the Poe Museum in Richmond, for answering my many questions and correcting my mistakes, and to Katarina Spears, executive director, for her interest in getting Edgar Allan Poe into Virginia classrooms; to Josh Gillespie, formerly director of preservation services at the Historic Richmond Foundation, for a fascinating tour of the Monumental Church, and to Katherine M. Gillespie for letting me know about the many Poe-related documents at the Library of Virginia in Richmond; to Jeff Jerome, curator of the Poe House in Baltimore, for sharing his insights when I visited and giving me a very useful copy of *Edgar Allan Poe: Literary Theory and Criticism*; to the E. A. Poe Society for its exhaustive Web site; to Helen McKenna-Uff, National Park Service ranger at the Edgar Allan Poe National Historic Site in Philadelphia, for her helpful suggestions; to the Bronx Historical Society for making possible my visit to Fordham Cottage; and to Michael Deas for generously sharing his expertise on the portraits and daguerreotypes of Poe. Thank you especially to my husband, Stuart Gagnon, and my children, Jeremy and Caroline, for their love, support, and encouragement while I wrote this book.

"Literature is the most noble of professions. In fact, it is about the only one fit for man ... I shall be a litterateur ... Nor would I abandon the hopes which still lead me on for all the gold in California."

— letter to Frederick
William Thomas
February 14, 1849

A bronze Poe leans forward as he listens to celestial music. The University of Baltimore School of Law statue was created by Sir Moses Jacob Ezekiel to celebrate the 1909 centennial of the author and poet's birth. An inscription reads: "To Thee The Laurels Belong, Best Bard, Whose Sweet Duty Was But to Sing."

FOREWORD

Dead men pilot a ship. An aristocrat walls his enemy inside a secret crypt. A murderer hears the heart of his victim beating beneath the floorboards. A royal party is broken up by a spectral figure dabbled in blood. An Inquisition victim watches helplessly as a razor-sharp pendulum swings toward him….

No author quite gets under a reader's skin like Edgar Allan Poe. His poems and tales can be wildly fanciful, but they are always psychologically truthful. He knew that, under the right circumstances, all of us can be tipped toward darkness, and he was brave enough to follow extreme states of mind—obsession, fear, rage—to their natural (and unnatural) ends.

You will learn much about Poe's sad life in this book, but there is a happy story to tell as well. The body of work he compiled, often against great odds, is still challenging and troubling and, yes, frightening us 200 years after his birth. No writer could ask for more.

Louis Bayard

Louis Bayard

Author of *The Pale Blue Eye*, a mystery
set during Poe's time at West Point

dgar Poe was not yet three when the world as he knew it ended. Since his birth in Boston on January 19, 1809, he had toured the East Coast with his mother, Elizabeth Arnold Poe, a beautiful and sweet-voiced actress, and his father, David Poe, Jr., a less popular performer. Edgar was surrounded by the rough-and-tumble life of the theater. Critics at that time were savage in their reviews of plays. Their words wounded Edgar's father, who went to the home of at least one reviewer to take him to task. Audiences were no more kind. They might hiss a performer off the stage. Actors worked long hours, not only entertaining audiences but also learning scores of parts. Yet actors were not well paid or respected. In New England, where the profession was seen as immoral, laws had been passed against putting on plays.

Little Edgar was still just learning to talk in this tough but familiar world, when a series of events unfolded as dark as any of the tales that would later make him famous. By August of 1811, Poe's father, a drinker, abandoned Edgar and his mother, along with Edgar's older brother, Henry, and his baby sister, Rosalie. Never rich, the family fell further into poverty. Then, in October in Richmond, Virginia, Edgar's mother became too sick to perform. She had tuberculosis, a deadly disease that destroys the lungs. Wealthy Richmond women came to her assistance, visiting the sick woman in her rented room

Soon after the two-year-old Poe's mother and father died, the Richmond (Virginia) Theatre, where both had acted, burned to the ground. The disaster took a horrifying toll in human lives and scattered the group of performers with which the little child had traveled. Poe and his siblings were sent to separate foster homes.

and providing nurses and food. Elizabeth's theater troupe staged benefits to raise money for her. But it was no use.

Edgar and Rosalie waited by their 24-year-old mother's bedside as she coughed up blood and struggled to breathe. An observer described the children as thin, pale, and fussy. According to one report, a nurse gave them bread soaked in gin to calm them. For weeks, Elizabeth Poe lingered on. Then, on December 8, she died. She was buried in an unmarked grave in St. John's Churchyard, in the section reserved for the poor.

Edgar was taken in by Frances Allan, one of the women who had helped his mother as she lay dying. She and her husband, John Allan, had no children. The boy was not formally adopted into their family, but he was baptized with their name: Edgar Allan Poe. His one-year-old sister, Rosalie, went to live with the MacKenzies, another well-to-do family in Richmond. His older brother, Henry, went to Baltimore, Maryland, to live with their grandparents — Elizabeth Cairnes Poe and "General" David Poe, Sr., a businessman who had helped supply American troops during the Revolutionary War. The three siblings were effectively left as orphans when their father either died or disappeared, never to be seen again.

For Christmas, Edgar traveled with his foster mother and father to a plantation down the James River from Richmond. While he was there, on December 26, the Richmond Theatre, the building where his mother had last performed, burned to the ground and 72 people died. Their remains were laid in the orchestra pit, which was hastily bricked up as a tomb. Grieving, the surviving members of Elizabeth Poe's theater troupe bade the city farewell.

Poe's mother, Elizabeth, was a pretty actress who audiences loved. Because she died when Poe was so young, he must have had few recollections of her, but she left him with this portrait and a note to remember Boston (background), the city where he was born and where she found good friends.

"In this miserable calamity we find a sentence of banishment," read a newspaper notice. Richmond went into mourning. Years later, Poe would connect the terrible events of that December in his mind. Asked about his background, he would say that his parents had perished with so many others in the Richmond Theatre fire.

Within the space of a month, everything upon which a small child depends had been taken from Poe. He was left with two objects: a miniature painting of his mother's girlish face — large-eyed and fringed by curls — and a watercolor

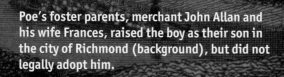

Poe's foster parents, merchant John Allan and his wife Frances, raised the boy as their son in the city of Richmond (background), but did not legally adopt him.

RICHMOND.

seen in the central part —

of Boston harbor. On this the dying woman wrote, "For my little son Edgar, who should ever love Boston, the place of his birth, and where his mother found her best, and most sympathetic, friends." Poe would cherish these mementos. When he was old enough, he would piece together the facts of his mother's and father's lives, dropping them like clues into the tales he wrote. The son of poor actors, never officially adopted into his foster parents' upper-class Richmond world, Poe would spend his life searching for, inventing, and defending who he was. Again and again, he would grapple with the mysteries of suffering and death.

As a young man of 20, he would write a poem that echoes the loss that must have been his earliest memory. "From childhood's hour I have not been as others were," it begins. "I have not seen as others saw — I could not bring my passions from a common spring … And all I loved — I loved alone."

At "the dawn" of his life, he wrote, there had appeared:

> *From every depth of good and ill*
> *The mystery which binds me still …*
> *From the lighting in the sky*
> *As it passed me flying by —*
> *From the thunder and the storm —*
> *And the cloud that took the form*
> *(When the rest of Heaven was blue)*
> *Of a demon in my view.*

As unfortunate as were his first years, for a time Poe lived a favored life. John and Frances "Fanny" Allan probably spoiled the little boy, the only child in the family. They lived over a store in the center of Richmond. Residents of the city remembered Edgar as "a lovely little fellow, with dark curls and brilliant eyes, dressed like a young prince." Frances was often sick, but she gave Edgar a mother's love. John Allan was a hardworking, no-nonsense businessman, a Scotch immigrant who was out to make his fortune. But his letters reveal affection for the boy, and he gave his foster son a gentleman's education — the type of schooling an upper-class boy was supposed to receive. Once the child of a mother dependent on charity, Edgar had become the foster son of a man who mixed with Virginia's aristocracy — the owners of tobacco plantations that were worked by hundreds of slaves. When Edgar went to worship in the new Monumental Episcopal Church, erected as a memorial on the site of the Richmond Theatre, he did not have to take the stairs to the balcony where the poor people sat. Instead, he walked into the main part of the sanctuary and sat in a pew his foster father had bought.

When Edgar was six, his foster father moved the family to London to do business there. Edgar was sent to English boarding schools, chief among them the Manor House, where he studied writing, spelling, geography, the Christian faith, French, Latin, and literature — a solid foundation for his later career as a writer. The school's atmosphere gave him a different sort of education. At the time, people liked to read Gothic tales — horror stories that featured characters struggling against evil in ancient castles and other gloomy, mysterious settings. To a boy with an active imagination, living in the Manor House's rambling old building was like entering one of these stories. He would later evoke this experience in his Gothic tale "William Wilson." This story describes the lifelong struggle between a man and his mysterious twin self — the narrator's conscience.

In 1820, because of the failure of his foster father's business venture, the family sailed back to Richmond. There Poe continued his schooling, including classes in math, and started acting in amateur plays — which his foster father disapproved of. He also wrote poetry — admiring verses addressed to girls and satires that made fun of boys he did not like. These got him attention, but otherwise he was a quiet boy with just a few good friends. One of those was his schoolmate Robert Stanard. Poe, then 14, developed a crush on the boy's 30-year-old mother — "the first, purely ideal love of my soul." Poe went often to visit Mrs. Stanard, who became a sort of replacement mother while Fanny Allan lay ill. Within a year, though, Mrs. Stanard died. Poe walked with Robert to visit her grave. Later, her memory would inspire Poe to write and rewrite one of his

As fond of athletic feats as he was of poetry, at age 15 Poe swam six miles in the James River, which flows through Richmond. He got a bad sunburn but became a legend among local boys.

most famous poems, giving his friend's mother a name out of Greek mythology:

Helen, thy beauty is to me
Like those Nicean barks of yore,
That gently, o'er a perfumed sea,
The weary, wayworn wanderer bore
To his own native shore.

The year Mrs. Stanard died, Poe was 15. That summer, to win a bet, he swam six miles in the James River — persevering despite the hot sun and strong currents. That fall, Poe, a lieutenant in the Junior Morgan Riflemen, a volunteer militia, was issued an actual gun from the armory. The Marquis de Lafayette, a French Revolutionary War hero who had known Poe's grandfather, invited the riflemen to serve as his honor guard during a visit to Richmond.

"My determination is at length taken—to leave your house and endeavor—to find some place in this wide world. This is not a hurried determination, but one on which I have long considered—and having so considered my resolution is unalterable."

—letter to John Allan
March 19, 1827 (age 18)

When Poe was a teenager, his foster father inherited a fortune and moved into this mansion in Richmond. Bitter quarrels with John Allan meant Poe would spend little time in the house, called Moldavia. Hoping for an inheritance, Poe instead received only meager allowances.

Poe fell in love with a neighborhood girl named Elmira Royster, but her father opposed their plans for marriage because Poe had little money and few prospects.

In school, Poe stood at the head of his class. But to his foster father he appeared to be an ungrateful boy who showed no affection toward the family that had taken him in and given him a fine education. "[He] does nothing [for me] & seems quite miserable, sulky, & ill-tempered," wrote Allan, who guessed that Poe had picked up his bad attitude from the wrong sort of friends.

As he neared adulthood, in 1825 at age 16, Poe was five foot eight inches tall and weighed 140 pounds — slender but athletic, with dark brown, curly hair, fair skin, fine features, and striking gray eyes. He wore long sideburns but not the moustache he would grow in his 30s. His voice was deep and melodious, and it carried a Southern accent. He had an animated face that neither he nor those who knew him felt portraits ever fully captured. He was polite and carried himself as he had been raised to — like a gentleman. He dressed carefully. His writing was small and neat.

Poe started spending time with Sarah Elmira Royster, a girl who lived several houses down from the Allans. They fell in love and wanted to get married. Her father, however, refused to grant his permission. Poe had not completed his education and had no money of his own.

John Allan had just inherited three quarters of a million dollars — the

Poe's foster father sent him to the University of Virginia in Charlottesville, where he lived in this room and struggled to pay expenses from the money John Allan provided. He gambled to get more cash and lost.

equivalent of almost $14.5 million today — from his uncle. He bought a mansion. But he was not about to lavish wealth on Poe. Instead, he sent his 17-year-old foster son to the University of Virginia in Charlottesville with very little money. Poe could only afford to enroll in two classes: Latin and French. He could not pursue his interest in math. The university, recently opened by Thomas Jefferson, was a wild place when Poe attended. There was a lot of drinking, gambling, and fighting. Poe got involved in all three but he also studied hard. He ranked high in both classes. During his spare time he entertained fellow students with his own short stories.

Poe, however, was falling deeply into debt. Owing Charlottesville merchants for basics like books and firewood, Poe gambled at cards to try to win money.

TAMERLANE

Q.	S.

ung heads are giddy, ... young hearts are warm
d make mistakes for manhood to reform.—Cowp

At the age of 18, Poe traveled to Boston, where he published a book of poems (background) written in the style of his hero, the English poet Lord Byron (portrait), who had died fighting in the Greek war for independence.

BOSTON:
CALVIN F. S. THOMAS.....PRINTER

....

1827.

Unfortunately, he lost. His foster father paid only some of what Poe owed for basics and not a penny of the gambling debts. These amounted to perhaps $2,000 — more than four times what he originally owed. John Allan told Poe he would have to leave the university.

Under threat of jail from creditors, Poe returned to Richmond to work as a clerk for his father. He discovered that Elmira Royster's father had intercepted the letters he sent to her from the university—and she would soon marry someone else. In March 1827, having just turned 18, Poe ran off to Boston, the city his mother had loved. There he arranged for his first volume of poetry, *Tamerlane and Other Poems*, to be published. He was paid in copies of the book. The title poem was about the great-grandson of Genghis Khan, a Mongol emperor who conquered half the globe. The title page of the slim book identified Poe only as "a Bostonian."

Poetry was, and would remain, Poe's ideal occupation — his lifelong passion. He likened it to music, eventually describing poetry as "The Rhythmical Creation of Beauty." As a teenager he imagined himself a glamorous figure like Lord Byron, the English aristocrat who wrote poems about the adventures of rebellious young men like himself. Byron died of a fever at the age of 36 while fighting for Greece's independence from Turkey. Like Byron and other "Romantics," Poe wanted to remake the world. The poem "Tamerlane" warns against ambition: Its hero tries so hard to become powerful that he loses what is important in life — love. Yet Poe himself was proud and ambitious. He wanted to become famous, to prove himself to his foster father (who was not a fan of Byron). And he believed that he could, by writing great poetry.

But Poe needed money. So he enlisted in the army, under the name Edgar A. Perry. "I have thrown myself on the world," he wrote his foster father, with romantic flourish. "I must either conquer or die. Succeed or be disgraced." As a humble private, surrounded by soldiers who hadn't had half his education, he served two years at Fort Independence in Massachusetts, Fort Moultrie in Charleston, South Carolina, and Fort Monroe near Norfolk,

Lacking a job, Poe enlisted in the army under the name Perry and was sent to Fort Monroe near Norfolk, Virginia, where he rose rapidly through the ranks as an artilleryman.

Virginia. Drawing on his background in mathematics, he mixed explosives for artillery shells. Later, he told people a much more exotic story: that he had volunteered to fight with the Greeks and had ended up in St. Petersburg, Russia.

Poe rose quickly in the army. He was promoted in 19 months to sergeant major, a position that normally took 20 years to reach. To rise further, he needed his foster father's help. When Fanny Allan died at the age of 44, Poe rushed back to Richmond, just missing the funeral. He and his foster father made peace with one another, and John Allan agreed to assist Poe with getting out of the army and into the United States Military Academy at West Point.

At that time, an enlisted man could leave the army early if he hired a substitute. Poe ended up promising the man who would replace him as a soldier $75 instead of the usual $12. He said his foster father would pay an IOU for $50. When John Allan did not pay the IOU, Poe wrote to the replacement that his foster father was often drunk. Fed up, the replacement sent Allan the letter. Poe's lie turned Allan against him once and for all.

At West Point in 1830, Poe studied mathematics and French and wrote poetry on the side—he collected money from his fellow cadets to publish another book. Once more, he excelled in his classes. But he could not win the approval of his foster father, who, as before, did not give him enough money to attend school. After John Allan remarried, he sent Poe a letter saying he no longer wished to hear from him. Struggling to pay his bills and impatient with military life, Poe decided to leave West Point. Allan failed to send the required letter of permission for Poe to leave, so Poe deliberately missed drills and classes and disobeyed rules so that he would be expelled. In March 1831 a court-martial dismissed him from the academy.

With books of poetry but little money to his name, Poe went to his father's poor relatives in Baltimore. The cramped household included his grandmother, Elizabeth Poe; his brother, Henry Poe — a drinker who soon died of tuberculosis at the age of 24 — his widowed aunt, Maria Clemm; her son, Henry, and her daughter, Virginia. The family paid the rent and other expenses with money Maria earned making dresses and with Elizabeth Poe's pension from Poe's grandfather's military service.

Poe came to depend on his new family. Poe's cousin, Virginia, eight, was 14 years younger than he was and had not been to school, though she had been taught to sing and to play the piano. Despite this the two developed a close friendship. Poe called Virginia "Sissy." She called him "Eddie." Virginia looked up to Poe, and he tutored her. They went for walks together. After a time, Virginia's mother began to treat

Broke and rejected by his foster father, Poe moved in with poor relatives in Baltimore, including his dead father's sister, his aunt Maria Clemm ("Muddy"). In the cramped house (background) where she cooked, cleaned, and sewed, Poe found love, security, and a place to write.

Poe like a son, and Poe started to behave toward his aunt as if she were his mother, calling her "Muddy." Poe wrote tales and entered literary contests. Maria cooked, cleaned, did the laundry, and often carried what Poe wrote to editors to sell.

Their efforts paid off. In October 1833, Poe won a $50 prize from the *Baltimore Saturday Visiter* for "MS. [Manuscript] Found in a Bottle," a tale inspired by that era's journeys of discovery: Captain Cook's exploration of the South Pacific, whaling voyages to the northern reaches of that ocean, and a planned American expedition to the frozen wastes of Antarctica. In the story, a sailor finds himself on a ghost vessel being sucked toward a dark whirlpool at the South Pole. At the last minute he throws a message overboard. The tale ends with his final words: "It is evident that we are hurrying onwards to some exciting knowledge—some never-to-be-imparted secret, whose attainment is destruction." This was the first of many tales Poe would write about fantastic journeys to the limits of discovery, whether to the ends of the Earth or to the farthest reaches of human knowledge. They are some of the earliest works of science fiction, one of today's most popular genres of literature.

In early 1834, John Allan fell seriously ill, and Poe traveled to Richmond to see him, still hoping for an inheritance. But Allan had already written Poe out of his will. When Allan died, he left his foster son nothing. Poe returned to Baltimore broke. After three years with little income from writing, his clothes were so worn that he was ashamed to accept invitations to have dinner in other people's homes.

Poe had to figure out how to make writing pay. Before the 1800s, most American writers came from wealthy families. During Poe's time, writers often survived on salaries as ministers, professors, or government officials.

Publishers gave American writers very little money for their works, because they could print famous European authors such as Charles Dickens for free. There was no copyright law to force publishers to pay foreign writers for their works. A few big-name, popular American authors like Washington Irving, who wrote the *Legend of Sleepy Hollow*, or James Fenimore Cooper, who wrote *The Last of the Mohicans*, were paid well, but most, like Poe, struggled.

Poe joined forces with English author and activist Charles Dickens to argue that writers should be paid more for their works.

In order to sell his works, Poe directed his writing to the newly emerging mass market. In early 19th-century America, for the first time, large numbers of people could read — and could afford to buy — the cheap magazines and books pouring from steam-driven printing presses. Poe chose topics that were in the news and on everybody's mind, such as exploration, hot-air balloon voyages, and solving puzzles — a public fascination since the ancient Egyptian writing system of hieroglyphics had just been deciphered by French scholar Champollion. To hook readers, Poe created suspense by tapping into readers' anxieties. He wrote about mistakenly being buried alive—a real possibility at a time when not even doctors could tell the difference between a person who was dead and one in a coma. He wrote about murder, a common event in growing cities that lacked police forces and had higher homicide rates than urban areas today. He wrote about disease, which was a fact of life, as yellow fever and other epidemics swept through crowded cities and tuberculosis took its slower, sadder toll as it spread through the coughs of victims. And, during a period when previous beliefs about life beyond the grave were breaking down in the face of science and reason, Poe wrote about death and what might come afterward.

Most important, as the idea that individuals were born basically good replaced the pre-1700s belief that people were born sinners, Poe wrestled with the problem of evil — of the animal, irrational side of human behavior and the powerful force exercised by the part of the brain we visit in our dreams (the unconscious). How was it possible that some individuals, for no reason that made any sense, committed horrible crimes? What was the force inside individuals that propelled them to act in ways that hurt not only others but also themselves? As Poe wrote in "The Imp of the Perverse," "We tremble with the violence of the conflict within us, — of the definite with the indefinite — of the substance with the shadow."

To grab readers and pull them through his stories, Poe carefully crafted what he wrote. He used every word to produce what he called a "single effect" on the reader, keeping stories as short and focused as possible. And he pioneered methods of telling incredible tales in believable ways. Sometimes he related them through a narrator who himself could scarcely accept what he had experienced. Other times he told them through a person who was pushed to the limits of sanity, dreaming, drunk, or under the influence of drugs.

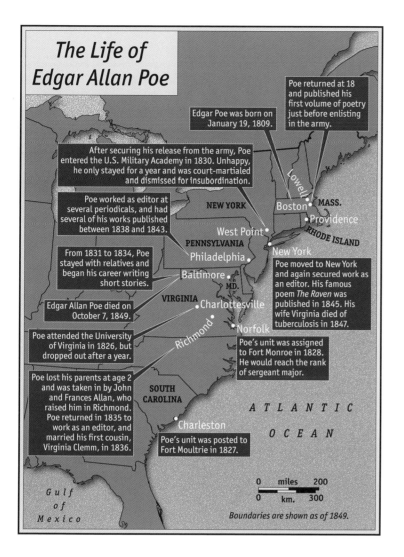

The Life of Edgar Allan Poe

Poe returned at 18 and published his first volume of poetry just before enlisting in the army.

Edgar Poe was born on January 19, 1809.

After securing his release from the army, Poe entered the U.S. Military Academy in 1830. Unhappy, he only stayed for a year and was court-martialed and dismissed for insubordination.

Poe worked as editor at several periodicals, and had several of his works published between 1838 and 1843.

From 1831 to 1834, Poe stayed with relatives and began his career writing short stories.

Edgar Allan Poe died on October 7, 1849.

Poe attended the University of Virginia in 1826, but dropped out after a year.

Poe lost his parents at age 2 and was taken in by John and Frances Allan, who raised him in Richmond. Poe returned in 1835 to work as an editor, and married his first cousin, Virginia Clemm, in 1836.

Poe moved to New York and again secured work as an editor. His famous poem *The Raven* was published in 1845. His wife Virginia died of tuberculosis in 1847.

Poe's unit was assigned to Fort Monroe in 1828. He would reach the rank of sergeant major.

Poe's unit was posted to Fort Moultrie in 1827.

Lowell • Boston • MASS. • Providence • RHODE ISLAND • West Point • NEW YORK • PENNSYLVANIA • Philadelphia • New York • Baltimore • MD. • VIRGINIA • Charlottesville • Richmond • Norfolk • SOUTH CAROLINA • Charleston

ATLANTIC OCEAN

Gulf of Mexico

0 miles 200
0 km. 300

Boundaries are shown as of 1849.

Poe spent most of his life in the fast-growing cities of America's industrializing East Coast — Richmond, New York, Baltimore, and Philadelphia. Their crowds, crime, and epidemics inspired many of his stories.

In "MS. Found in a Bottle," he presented his tale through a diary fished from the sea. So successful was Poe at making the unbelievable seem possible, the most convincing of his stories were accepted as actual news accounts. Poe love pulling off these hoaxes. He played with his audience by filling his tales with riddles and mixing fiction and fact.

Yet despite his growing skill as a short story writer, Poe still could not pay the bills. So in 1835 he moved to Richmond to become editor at the *Southern Literary Messenger*. His salary: $10 a week — around $215 in today's money.

Soon after, Eliza Poe died, cutting off the pension that had supported her, Maria, and Virginia. Poe invited Virginia and Muddy to live with him in Richmond. But Neilson Poe, a well-to-do cousin of Poe's and Virginia's, invited Virginia to stay in his Baltimore home and attend school. Afraid of losing both

"For Virginia, my love, my own sweetest Sissy, my darling little wifey, think well before you break the heart of your poor cousin, Eddy."

August 29, 1835

Despite Poe's being 14 years older than his Baltimore cousin, the writer (shown as he looked around age 37) and Virginia (shown in a death portrait at age 24) were married in Richmond. Poe was 27 and Virginia was just 13 (marriage certificate, background).

Virginia and her mother, Poe begged Maria Clemm to come to Richmond: "My last my last my only hold on life is cruelly torn away. What have I *to live for*? Among strangers with *not one soul to love me*." He began to drink.

It was the first of many times that Poe would react to troubles by turning to alcohol. And it was the first of many times that a drinking binge would lead him to neglect his work and lose the trust of employers and friends. Poe was not a social drinker who had one or two drinks with friends over dinner or at a party, all the while engaging in polite conversation. Instead, he became intoxicated quickly, and when in that state was out of control — a completely different person than when sober. During dark periods in his life, Poe drank to get drunk, hoping to enter a kind of oblivion. In short, Poe, like his father and brother, abused alcohol. He only managed to produce as much work as he did because of long periods when he did not drink.

"I have absolutely no pleasure in the stimulants in which I sometimes so madly indulge," he wrote later in his life. "It has not been in the pursuit of pleasure that I have periled life and reputation and reason. It has been the desperate attempt to escape from torturing memories, a sense of insupportable loneliness, a dread of some strange impending doom."

Eventually, Virginia and her mother accepted Poe's invitation and moved into the Richmond boardinghouse where he lived. Poe and Virginia were married in 1836. He was 27. She was 13. With a family to support, Poe set about making a name for himself through his reviews for the *Messenger*.

At this time, many people were urging Americans to read American writers just because they were Americans. Poe, though patriotic, ridiculed the idea: "[We]

As a literary critic out to make a name for himself, Poe savaged American writers in reviews written at this desk for Richmond's *Southern Literary Messenger*. The writer James Russell Lowell (above) praised Poe's reviews.

often find ourselves … liking a stupid book the better, because, sure enough, its stupidity is American." The young country could develop better writers, Poe argued, if reviewers celebrated those few who showed exceptional talent and harshly criticized the many who did not. He especially objected to the common practice of reviewers praising mediocre writers who were their friends or who had paid them money—a practice known as "puffing."

In one of many savage critiques, Poe tore apart *Norman Leslie*, a novel by Theodore S. Fay, who had many friends among editors and reviewers in New York. "We do not mean to say that there is positively nothing in Mr. Fay's novel to commend—but there is indeed very little. … The plot … is a monstrous piece of absurdity. … The characters have no character at all. … The hero … [is] a great fool. … As regards Mr. Fay's style, it is unworthy of a school-boy."

Poe, the southern outsider, was attacking the country's literary establishment—a small clique of men in the North who controlled what was published. Many reacted positively.

Writer James Russell Lowell called Poe "the most discriminating, philosophical, and fearless … critic in America." Others took offense. "The greatest number [of his reviews] have been flippant, unjust, untenable, and uncritical … [filled with] sneers, sarcasm, and downright abuse," wrote William Leese Stone of the *New York Commercial Advertiser*.

Poe did not relent. He was becoming a literary celebrity; people called him the "tomahawk [hatchet] man." He was also making powerful enemies, who would look for an opportunity to "scalp" him.

Poe's quarrels with the North extended to abolitionists—those who wanted to get rid of slavery. Though Poe was not necessarily a supporter of the cruelties of slavery (and avoided making direct statements on the controversial issue), he thought the abolitionists were fanatical extremists. He resented their imposing their opinions on the South. In general, he was suspicious of "progress"—the idea that modern political, social, and technological changes were making the world a better place. While others praised America's democracy, Poe worried about mob rule by the ignorant, gullible masses.

The harsh tone of Poe's reviews earned him a nickname, the "tomahawk man," and made him the butt of jokes, as in this 1849 cartoon.

With his newfound national reputation, Poe was asked by a New York publisher to write what turned out to be his first and only novel. *The Narrative of A. Gordon Pym* recounts a young man's horrific adventures during an accidental journey to Antarctica. Like many novels of that time, it was written as a serial — a series of chapters published in a magazine over weeks or months. Just as the first installments appeared in the *Messenger*, Poe fought with the magazine's owner. He was tired of working in what he called "the magazine prison house," doing tedious work while his employer enjoyed the profits. Fired in early 1837, Poe traveled to New York with his family, looking for a position in the center of the publishing world. But there were no jobs. A financial crisis launched an economic depression that would last for the next seven years. The family survived on bread and molasses.

Poe moved again with his family, this time to Philadelphia, where they remained poor. *Pym* was published in book form in 1838 but brought Poe no money. So Poe focused once more on short stories, and wrote many of his most famous, including "The Fall of the House of Usher." In this Gothic tale, a man is summoned by an eccentric friend to a bizarre, decaying mansion to witness the final days of the friend and the friend's dying twin sister.

Some readers interpret "Usher" as an account of the disintegration of a person's

In Philadelphia, where Poe took another editing job, Virginia showed the first signs of the dreaded disease tuberculosis. She struggled to sleep in this bedroom, as she coughed to clear her failing lungs. Poe, who had watched his mother die of the same sickness, could do nothing.

Poe's Gothic short story, "The Fall of the House of Usher" ends with the collapse of a doomed family's decaying mansion. Some say the house's ruin is a metaphor for inner conflicts that can tear a person apart.

mind. Others group the story with a half dozen others Poe wrote about dying or dead women who break out of tombs and come back from the dead. In the "Philosophy of Composition," Poe wrote that there was no subject more poetic than "the death … of a beautiful woman." He was not alone in choosing this topic—lots of authors wrote about beautiful women who died young of tuberculosis, a disease that claimed many victims in their 20s, turning them rosy-cheeked at the very end. The dead women in Poe's stories, however, don't stay in the grave.

In the 1841 tale, "The Murders in the Rue Morgue," a brilliant man discovers the unlikely killer of two women. The story was quickly reprinted (background) and inspired a 1932 movie (poster). With it, Poe invented detective fiction.

Biographer Kenneth Silverman, in *Edgar Allan Poe: Mournful and Never-Ending Remembrance*, sees these stories as evidence that Poe never got over the loss of his mother at age two. He argues that Poe, because he was so young, never fully accepted the idea that his mother was dead, not to return. Other scholars say that because of the early death of his mother, Poe idealized women — depicting them as perfect and strong enough to conquer death. These scholars point out that Poe's male characters often commit terrible violence against women (for example, Roderick Usher seals his sister alive in the family vault). Poe's men, they say, are trying to free themselves from being dependent on women, much as a child breaks away from his or her parents in order to become an adult.

In 1841, Poe invented a different sort of character in whom scholars see the author himself: C. Auguste Dupin. An aristocrat and eccentric genius fallen on hard times, Dupin uses meticulous reasoning and intuition — gut feelings or sudden understanding — to solve mysteries. He is the first ever fictional detective, and the story in which he makes his appearance, "The Murders in the Rue Morgue," is the first detective story, another of today's popular literary genres. The term didn't exist back then, so Poe called it a tale of "ratiocination," or rational thinking. In it, Dupin figures out how two women have been brutally murdered in a locked room, a crime that has stumped the police. Poe would write several more such stories, including "The Gold Bug," which won him a $100 prize and was the most popular of Poe's tales during his lifetime. The hero of that story must decipher a secret code in order to find a buried treasure.

Already the success of stories like "MS. Found in a Bottle" had persuaded a publisher to print the first collection of Poe's work, *Tales of the Grotesque and Arabesque*. But his payment was only 20 free copies. In order to feed his family, Poe took positions first as an assistant editor at *Burton's Gentlemen's Magazine*, then as an editor at its successor, *Graham's Magazine*. At *Graham's* Poe's output and reputation grew, though he was only paid $800 a year — the equivalent of around $18,000 today. He praised rising authors Charles Dickens and Nathaniel Hawthorne in reviews. All the while, he dreamed of owning his own magazine. The first name he came up with was *The Penn*. Then he decided on *The Stylus*.

In January 1842, Poe was relaxing at home with his beloved family when the dread disease that had taken his mother stole into his parlor. Virginia, who had been singing, cut off suddenly and began to spit up blood. She had burst a blood vessel — a sure sign of tuberculosis. From that day on, Virginia would be sick, and Poe would watch, helpless, as she slowly died. He would listen, pained, to her agonized coughs. Sometimes her health improved, but never for long. The fatal disease always returned.

Once more, Poe resorted to alcohol. "I became insane, with long intervals of horrible sanity," he later described it. "During these fits of absolute unconsciousness I drank, God only knows how often or how much."

That spring, Poe wrote a short, devastating tale, "The Masque of the Red Death." In the story, the "red death," a terrible sickness whose victims die covered in blood, slips into the castle where a prince has retreated to wait out the epidemic. In a moment, the ruler and all his court perish. No one escapes death.

Frustrated with the "namby pamby" nature of *Graham's*, which was not sophisticated enough for his taste, and fed up with his low pay, Poe quit the magazine. He looked for another job, including a civil service position with the government, but could find nothing. He failed to raise the money to start his own magazine. So he eked out a living freelancing and lecturing on American poetry to sell-out crowds.

Poe's ambitions remained, though. In 1844, he again moved his family to New York City, where he took a job at the *Evening Mirror*. The next year he published the poem that made him an instant celebrity and remains one of the most famous ever: "The Raven." In the poem, a man grieving for his dead love, Lenore, is visited by a raven that speaks, but one word only: "Nevermore." Poe's deft rhymes and masterful use of meter make the verses linger in readers' memories. The poem was reprinted again and again. Poe received just $15 for its first appearance.

Now 36, Poe was at the peak of his career. He became coeditor and then

Out to challenge the northern literary establishment, Poe attacked the famous poet Henry Wadsworth Longfellow (left) again and again, accusing him of plagiarism. Longfellow did not strike back, but a little-known editor, Rufus Griswold (right), who took offense at some of Poe's other reviews, would later wreck the writer's reputation.

owner of *The Broadway Journal*. But like the narrator of "The Raven," he was soon beset by "unmerciful disaster [which] followed fast and followed faster." In order to boost the *Journal's* circulation, he relentlessly attacked the New England poet Henry Wadsworth Longfellow whom he accused of plagiarism — copying the work of others. Poe's old friend Lowell turned against him, implying that Poe had stolen the idea of a talking raven from a Dickens novel: "Here comes Poe with his Raven, like Barnaby Rudge — Three-fifths of him genius, and two-fifths sheer fudge."

In "The Raven," the poem that brought Poe his greatest fame (but little money), a gloomy blackbird (background) flies into the bedroom of a grieving man (engraving) and will not leave, trapping him beneath its dark shadow (staged in a play) and dooming him to a life of endless mourning.

"Deep into that darkness peering,
long I stood there wondering, fearing,

Doubting, dreaming dreams no mortal
ever dared to dream before ..."

—from "The Raven"

Even where Poe had better grounds for his negative reviews, he was making enemies. Poe criticized some of the work of Rufus Griswold, a mediocre author who specialized in issuing collections of other writers' work. He also found fault with the work of one of Griswold's friends. This left Griswold looking for revenge. Unwisely, years later Poe made Griswold his literary executor — the person charged with publishing his works after he died.

As a celebrity, Poe was invited to literary salons — parties for writers in wealthy people's homes. There he attracted admiring women, including many aspiring poets. He became close with one of these, Frances Osgood, the wife of a painter. Poe and Osgood were devoted friends and published platonic love poems to each other. Frances and Virginia became friends as well and spent a lot of time together. One day, another of Poe's admirers, a married woman named Elizabeth Ellett, visited Poe's house to find Frances and Virginia laughing at the love letters Ellett had sent Poe. Angry, Ellett accused Osgood of writing things to Poe that no married woman should. When he heard of it, Poe said that Ellett should worry instead about what she had been writing to him—and returned Ellett's letters. In the ensuing confusion, Ellett's brother threatened to kill Poe, and the city's leading hostesses took Poe off the guest lists for their parties.

Meanwhile, a literary feud between Poe and writer Thomas Dunn English — Poe made fun of English's poems and English ridiculed Poe in a novel — degenerated into an actual brawl, with punches thrown. Poe continued the fight in a series of magazine articles called the "Literati of New York City," which included an unflattering portrait of Dunn. Dunn retaliated with a newspaper article that portrayed Poe as the villain in the Ellett affair, accusing him of forgery, and calling him a "thoroughly unprincipled, base and depraved" drunk. Poe sued for libel and eventually won. But the damage was done—his name was associated with scandal.

Early in 1846, Virginia had written Poe a Valentine's Day poem pleading for a peaceful, private life in a cottage far from the gossip of New York City:

Love alone shall guide us when we
are there—
Love shall heal my weakened lungs …

Several months later, shortly after *The Broadway Journal* failed and just as Dunn was publishing his attack, Edgar, Virginia, and Muddy moved from downtown New York 13 miles north to Fordham. The village, now in the Bronx, lay outside the boundaries of the city. Poe negotiated a low rent on a worker's cottage near the newly completed train line. Surrounded by fields and orchards, with a view from the hills down to Long Island Sound, the cozy little one-and-a-half-story house provided

While Virginia lay sick at home, Poe, now a celebrity in New York City, attended parties at which he was surrounded by women admirers, including the poet Frances Osgood, above. The two exchanged poems and love letters, like this Valentine from Poe (background).

Poe's relations with society women had gotten him into trouble, he was low on money, and Virginia was growing weaker, so the writer moved his family out of the city to this cottage in what was then the quiet village of Fordham. The Poes loved living out in the country, but Virginia's health continued to deteriorate. She died in January 1847, leaving Poe, who was himself ill, devastated with grief.

a retreat from the city. The family hoped the clean air would help Virginia. But Poe fell ill and could not work. Virginia's health grew worse. She lay suffering from the chills on a straw mattress in a tiny bedroom downstairs. Lacking even money for blankets, the family tried to keep Virginia warm under Poe's heavy overcoat and the family's cat, Catterina. A visitor to the cottage in November spread the word about the Poes' misery. Newspapers ran stories. Soon Virginia had a donated feather bed to sleep on and the attentions of a kind nurse named Marie Louise Shew. However, it was too late. On January 30, 1847—about five years after she had shown the first symptom of the disease—Virginia died of tuberculosis. She was 24 years old, the same age that Poe's mother had been. Shew paid for a coffin and linen grave clothes.

Poe was overcome with sadness. The normally prolific author who had so often written about grief and loss could now barely write two lines. Again, he fell sick. When he was well enough, he took long walks. Once, he hiked 12 miles northeast to Mamaroneck, where he found an avenue of pine trees that led to an old cemetery. The setting inspired one of his most acclaimed poems, "Ulalume," about a grief-stricken man who mistakenly wanders to his beloved's tomb.

> *The skies they were ashen and sober;*
> *The leaves they were crisped and sere —*
> *The leaves they were withering and sere;*
> *It was night in the lonesome October*
> *Of my most immemorial year …*

Poe sold the poem, considered one of his greatest, for little more than the price of a pair of shoes — he had split his old pair in a leaping contest with friends and had nothing to wear on his bare feet.

Despite his poverty and grief, Poe was not always the tortured soul people expected from his poetry and press accounts. Five months after Virginia died, Mary Elizabeth Bronson went with her father, an Episcopal minister and professor of public speaking, to visit the now famous author. "We saw Mr. Poe walking in his yard, and most agreeably was I surprised to see a very handsome and elegant appearing gentleman who welcomed us with a quiet, cordial, and graceful politeness," she wrote. "I dare say I looked the surprise I felt, for I saw an amused look on his face as I raised my eyes [to his]." Poe joked around, apologizing that he didn't have a pet raven.

"Deep in earth my love is lying
And I must weep alone."

—couplet Poe wrote in early 1847,
just after his wife, Virginia, died

An imagined scene shows Poe
walking alone at midnight
across the bridge near his home
in Fordham. Throughout his life,
Poe took hikes to clear his mind.
After Virginia's death, the writer
roamed the countryside, trying
to deal with the pain.

"To the few who love and whom I love—to those who feel rather than those who think—to the dreamers and those who put faith in dreams as the only realities ... What I here propound is true:—therefore it cannot die ..."

—dedication to *Eureka*, 1848

Poe sat for a portrait in New York City six months after his wife's death. Many believe this is that photo. If so, it is the last picture in which the 38-year-old writer, who was struggling with depression and a drinking problem, appears in good health.

In January 1848, nearing the one-year anniversary of his wife's death, Poe began work on *Eureka* (Greek for "I have found it"), a 150-page essay that tackles the biggest mysteries of all: Where did we come from? Where are we going? In the beginning, Poe wrote, God/the universe was a single particle. Then the Divine Being willed itself to expand, growing bigger and bigger, and separating into many individual creatures. The universe would eventually shrink back to its original size and unity. *Eureka* reminds some today of the Big Bang theory—the scientific idea that the universe began 14 billion years ago with a huge explosion, expanding from a tiny particle to fill all of space in every direction. But *Eureka*'s message was the truth of poems: Death is an illusion. And after we perish, we return to the Divine Being, who is everywhere. "All is Life," Poe wrote, "Life—Life within Life."

Poe gave passionate lectures on *Eureka*, but it sold poorly. And his ideas, which seemed to contradict the Bible, scared off Shew, a devout Christian. For all his faith in the "Divine Being," Poe was falling apart—and he knew it. "Unless some true and tender and pure womanly love save me, I shall hardly last a year longer, alone!" he wrote Shew in June 1848, as he pleaded for her to remain his friend. The dozen surviving authentic images of Poe tell the story of his deterioration during and after his wife's illness and death. An acquaintance who saw him in 1846 said Poe was "evidently committing a suicide on his body." Within five years he went from a young, healthy man, with an intense but controlled gaze, to a much aged man, worn down from suffering, whose eyes spoke sadness.

In desperation, he attached himself to women, as he looked for someone

to save him. He exchanged poems with Sarah Helen Whitman (called Helen), a wealthy widow and poet who admired his verses. In September 1848, he traveled to her home in Providence, Rhode Island, to introduce himself. Soon after, he proposed marriage. Helen, six years older than Poe, was attracted to the writer but troubled by bad reports about his character and by her mother's and sister's strong objections to the match. So she turned down Poe's offer, saying she was too old and in poor health. Unable to get her to accept, on November 5 Poe attempted to kill himself. He took an overdose of a powerful drug called laudanum — a form of opium then available without a prescription for toothaches and diarrhea. Fortunately, he couldn't keep it down. Poe vomited up the drug and, when he recovered, proposed to Helen again. At one point, desperately persistent, he visited Helen's house drunk, begged her to rescue him from a "terrible, impending doom," grabbed at her, and tore a piece from her dress. Finally, on November 13, Mrs. Whitman relented. She and Poe were engaged on the condition that he not take another drink.

"No person could long be near him in his healthier moods, without loving him & putting faith in the sweetness & goodness of his nature," Helen Whitman later wrote. "But … how slight a wound could disturb his serenity, how trivial a disappointment could unbalance his whole being."

Poe's emotions at this time, as revealed in his letters, were extremely confused. At the same time he was courting Mrs. Whitman, Poe was professing his love for a married woman named Annie L. Richmond, who lived in Lowell, Massachusetts, and who had met Poe when he lectured there in July 1848. Mrs. Richmond's husband knew about the relationship. All three viewed it as a platonic friendship rather than a love affair. But Poe's feelings for Annie ran deep. He called her "wife of my soul." He relied on her companionship and the knowledge of her affection to keep himself going. "So long as I think that you know I love you, as no man ever loved a woman — so long as I think you comprehend in some measure, the fervor with which I adore you, so long, no worldly trouble can ever render me absolutely wretched," he wrote her shortly after he tried to kill himself. When Poe was engaged to Helen

Poe met Annie L. Richmond when he lectured in Lowell, Massachusetts, and the two developed a deep friendship that helped him cope with grief and loneliness. Poe's letters to her are filled with professions of love and pleas for her presence.

Whitman, he asked Annie if he and Muddy could move into a cottage close to her where he could see her and her family daily. "Think — oh *think* for me — before ... the vows are spoken, which put yet another terrible *bar*, between us ... Can you, *my* Annie, *bear* to think I am another's? ... I am so *ill* — so terribly, hopelessly ILL in body and mind that I feel I CANNOT live, unless I feel your sweet, gentle, loving hand pressed upon my forehead."

Poe did not move to Massachusetts to be with Annie. Neither did he marry Helen Whitman. She broke off their engagement two days before Christmas — their wedding day — after she learned he had been drinking. But Poe revived enough to resume working. In March 1849 he sent Mrs. Richmond a poem, "For Annie," praising the love that pulled him through the crisis.

The sickness — the nausea —
    The pitiless pain —
Have ceased, with the fever
    That maddened my brain —
with the fever called "Living"
    That burned in my brain.

Two months later, Poe mailed Annie the last poem he would ever write — "Annabel Lee." Some say it is about his love for Virginia. Helen Whitman claimed it was about his love for her. Other women, including Annie, have also been named as the real-life Annabel Lee. In the poem, a boy and a girl fall in love so deeply that the angels become jealous. A cold wind blows from Heaven, and the girl falls sick and dies. Yet the boy's passion for her does not end. He goes to sleep

Annabel Lee.

By Edgar A. Poe.

It was many and many a yea
   In a kingdom by the sea
That a maiden there lived who
   By the name of Annabe
And this maiden she lived wit
   Than to love and be love

She was a child and I was
   In this kingdom by the
But we loved with a love that
   I and my Annabel Lee
With a love that the winged ser
   Coveted her and me.

In the poem "Annabel Lee," shown here in a rare handwritten manuscript, Poe writes about passions so strong that a grieving boy goes to lie in the tomb of his dead love. Many believe Annabel Lee is really Virginia, a lock of whose long hair lies next to Poe's short hair in a framed keepsake.

And this was the reason that, long ago,
   In this kingdom by the sea,
A wind blew out of a cloud, chilling
   My beautiful Annabel Lee —
So that her high-born kinsmen came
   And bore her away from me,
To shut her up in a sepulchre

Back in the city of his childhood, Poe resumed courting his long-ago sweetheart, who was now Elmira Royster Shelton, a rich widow living in a fine Richmond home (background). After Poe swore off drinking, she agreed to marry him.

beside Annabel Lee in her tomb.

But our love it was stronger by far than
   the love
      Of those who were older than we —
      Of many far wiser than we —
And neither the angels in heaven above,
      Nor the demons down under the sea,
Can ever dissever my soul from the soul
Of the beautiful ANNABEL LEE.

In June 1849, Poe said goodbye to Muddy in New York City and took a train to Philadelphia, where friends said he misplaced his luggage, drank, was jailed briefly, and appeared to be losing his mind. About a month later, having recovered and begged enough money to continue his journey, Poe took the train to his planned destination, Richmond. There he checked in to a hotel and began renewing old friendships. After more than 20 years, he resumed courting his childhood sweetheart Elmira, now Elmira Royster Shelton and a rich widow. Poe lectured in Richmond and nearby Norfolk. He wore an embroidered silk vest and socks and drew crowds that he claimed earned him up to $100 a night. Determined to start anew, he swore off alcohol and joined the Sons of Temperance, whose members pledged not to drink. He and Elmira became engaged.

As the summer ended, Poe prepared to travel north to meet a woman who wanted him to edit her poetry and to get Muddy to come back to Richmond with him for the wedding. He had plans to go on a lecture tour to raise money to finally launch *The Stylus*. A wealthy editor of an Illinois weekly newspaper had written Poe pledging his support. The night of September 26, when Poe bid farewell to Elmira, he had a fever. He stopped at a doctor's house and, when he departed, took the doctor's cane instead of his own. Then he caught a steamboat to Baltimore at 4 a.m. on September 27.

Decked out in this embroidered silk vest, Poe lectured to sell-out audiences while in Richmond.

What happened next is unclear. For five days, Poe's exact whereabouts are unknown. Maybe he started drinking again. He was found October 3 in Baltimore, at a tavern being used as a polling place in local elections. He was incoherent, dirty, and dressed in someone else's cheap clothes (presumably, somebody stole his more expensive wool suit). A friend took him to a hospital, where he lingered for four days. Then early on October 7 he died. He was 40 years old. His final words: "Lord help my poor soul."

Planning to return to Richmond for his wedding with Elmira, Poe left his trunk behind when he departed the city on a steamship September 26, 1849, on his way to pursue an editing job and get his beloved aunt Muddy from Fordham. Then he disappeared — his whereabouts are unknown for the next five days.

"I have been so ill. The very instant you get this, come to me. The joy of seeing you will almost compensate for our sorrows. We can but die together. I must die. I have no desire to live since I have done 'Eureka.'"

—letter to Maria
Clemm (Muddy)
July 7, 1849

This photo, taken in Richmond, is the last picture of Poe, who was found October 3 in Baltimore, barely conscious in a tavern being used as an election polling place in the city's Fells Point section (background shows the doorway of a neighborhood bar). Poe was carried to a hospital, but died soon after.

1626 THAMES

"The Poe character, a man of acute faculties, a man of cool nerves, a man whose ardent but patient will hurls defiance at obstacles ... —this is Poe himself."

— Charles Baudelaire,
after Poe's death

There are dozens of theories about why Poe died. Since no autopsy was performed, and given the limited medical knowledge of the time, we will never know. Maybe he drank himself to death. Perhaps he was beaten by robbers. It could be he succumbed to heart disease or diabetes. Certain of his symptoms point to rabies or epilepsy — or mercury poisoning. It's possible that doses of the liquid metal given to prevent cholera drove him crazy. Soon after Poe's death, people started to speculate that he had been drugged and forced to cast fraudulent votes in the local elections. Later, they wondered whether Elmira's brothers got him intoxicated so the engagement would be called off.

Whatever killed Poe, now that he was dead, Poe's rival Griswold saw his chance for revenge. Griswold, who still felt slighted by Poe's reviews, submitted an obituary for the author and signed with a false name: "Edgar Allan Poe is dead … This announcement will startle many, but few will be grieved by it. The poet was well known … but he had few or no friends." Griswold described Poe as a lunatic who wandered the streets in storms talking to spirits. As a reviewer, Griswold wrote, about all Poe was good at was picking apart people's grammar.

Griswold's obituary was reprinted again and again. But the man Poe had trusted with his legacy was not done betraying him. First Griswold destroyed some of Poe's letters. Then he forged others. Finally, in the 1850s, he issued Poe's works with an even more damaging account of Poe's life. In this way, Griswold single-handedly wrecked Poe's reputation. Long afterward, editors and writers drew on Griswold's words for "facts" about Poe. Although friends published articles in Poe's defense, it would take many decades and much research before Griswold's lies were replaced with the truth.

AFTERWORD

We know him as Edgar Allan Poe, one of America's most popular, celebrated, and notorious writers. A doomed genius whose somber face stares out from T-shirts. A poet whose most famous work, "The Raven," provided the name for Baltimore's National Football League team. A writer who, 200 years after his birth, still speaks to kids in middle and high school. A legendary figure whose life has been the inspiration for mystery novels, pop and classical music, paintings, and struggling artists. Also, one of the country's most controversial authors. A writer who for generations some critics have rejected. A man whose works and life have at times been branded evil.

After his death, Poe was adopted as a hero, a saint, and a martyr by poet Charles Baudelaire and a succession of other French writers. These "Symbolists" appreciated the way he used dreamlike images to evoke the inner world of the human mind—a realm of conflicting emotions and little-understood impulses. They also admired the way he suffered for art. Poe's detective, C. Auguste Dupin, became a model for Arthur Conan Doyle's Sherlock Holmes and for every other fictional sleuth since. Poe's chilling tales influenced a long line of writers, including H. P. Lovecraft, who credited Poe with perfecting the modern horror story. Even T. S. Eliot, a 20th-century American poet who didn't particularly like

Each year on January 19, the anniversary of Poe's birth, people bring flowers to the grave in Baltimore where he is buried, along with Virginia and Muddy. In early morning darkness, a mysterious man leaves an elegant tribute: gifts and three roses.

Poe's work, had to admit his predecessor's importance: "And yet one cannot be sure that one's writing has not been influenced by Poe."

As a magazine editor and reviewer, Poe denounced mediocrity and promoted talent in a young, proud nation looking for its identity. As a poet, he wrote haunting, melodic poetry about love and death. As a short story writer, he helped give birth to science fiction. His keen mind invented the detective story. And his imagination produced tales of horror that confront us with our deepest fears — terrors that come not from the supernatural world of ghosts and vampires, but from the evil that lies within each of us.

Poe is often accused of being a pessimist. After all, he wrote about doomed,

A football mascot dressed as a raven celebrates Poe's memory in Baltimore. Proud of the great author who lived — and died — in their city, residents named their NFL team the Ravens, after Poe's most famous poem. More than 150 years after his death, Poe enjoys unrivalled popularity for a 19th-century author.

trapped characters, about murder, insanity, and death. He did not believe in progress or challenging the institution of slavery that was poisoning America. Where in Poe is optimism?

It can be found in the choices Poe made against all odds, in his ambition — to become a great writer, to transform American literature, to take on the most powerful editors in the country, to attempt in 150 pages to explain everything. It can be seen in the careful and disciplined labors he carried out in the midst of poverty, debt, sickness, the deaths of those he loved, slander, and mortal struggles with alcohol and despair. It is behind his continued remaking of himself. At the end, he was still hopeful. Ready to remarry. Ready to launch his own magazine. Ready to set to work again.

Poe set out in search of the limits of knowledge and discovery, hoping to unlock the mysteries of life and death. It was a harrowing journey, but Poe pressed on. Poet Walt Whitman had a vision of the writer's outrageous determination: "In a dream … I saw a vessel on the sea, at midnight, in a storm … now flying

uncontroll'd with torn sails and broken spars
through the wild sleet and winds and waves
of the night. On the deck was a slender, slight,
beautiful figure, a dim man, apparently enjoying
all the terror, the murk and the dislocation of
which he was the centre and the victim. That
figure … might stand for Edgar Poe."

Poe lives on in a variety of merchandise, including (left to right) a knickknack, an action figure, and a toy. The writer's haunting poems and riveting tales, as well as his own dark, tumultuous life make him the subject of continuing fascination. He has become a symbol of all artists who suffer for their work.

January 18, 1809 Born in Boston to actors Elizabeth Arnold Poe and David Poe, Jr.

December 8, 1811 Mother dies of tuberculosis in Richmond. Taken in by John and Frances Allan.

1815 The Allans move to London. Poe attends English boarding schools.

1820 The Allans return to Richmond, where Poe soon composes his first poems.

1825 Courts neighbor Elmira Royster until her father orders him to stop. Quarrels with John Allan, who has inherited a fortune.

1826 Sent to University of Virginia.

1827 Forced to leave school after John Allan refuses to pay his debts. Runs away to Boston. Publishes his first book, *Tamerlane and Other Poems*. Enlists in army.

1829 Foster mother dies. Arranges his own discharge from army.

1830 Enters U.S. Military Academy at West Point.

1831 Gets himself expelled from West Point. Moves in with relatives including aunt, Maria Clemm, and cousin, Virginia, in Baltimore. Starts writing full time.

1833 Early science fiction tale "MS. Found in a Bottle" wins prize.

1834 John Allan dies and leaves Poe nothing.

1835 Moves to Richmond to work as publisher's assistant at *Southern Literary Messenger*. Courts Virginia and suffers emotional crisis when he fears she will not marry him. Convinces Virginia and her mother to join him in Richmond.

1836 Marries 13-year-old Virginia. Makes reputation writing reviews and essays.

1837 Fired from the *Messenger* after bouts of drinking and arguments with publisher. Moves family to New York City, but cannot find work there.

1838 Moves to Philadelphia. Publishes his only novel, *The Narrative of Arthur Gordon Pym*.

1839 Becomes assistant editor of *Burton's Gentlemen's Magazine*. Publishes horror tales including "The Fall of the House of Usher" and his first book of short stories, *Tales of the Grotesque and Arabesque*.

1840 Dismissed from *Burton's* as he tries to start his own magazine.

1841 Joins *Graham's Magazine*. Publishes first modern detective story: "Murders in the Rue Morgue."

1842 Resumes drinking after Virginia coughs up blood—a sign of tuberculosis. Resigns from *Graham's*.

1844 Moves to New York City. Works for the *Evening Mirror*.

1845 Launches the short-lived *Broadway Journal*. Achieves greatest celebrity with his poem, "The Raven."

1846 Dogged by scandals and short of money, moves to Fordham, north of New York City. Takes to his bed with illness as Virginia herself approaches death.

January 30, 1847 Virginia dies. Poe falls into depression.

1848 Publishes *Eureka*, an explanation of everything. Pursues passionate but platonic love affair with Mrs. Annie Richmond of Lowell, Mass. Courts Sarah Helen Whitman in Providence, R.I. Attempts suicide when she refuses to marry him.

1849 Becomes engaged in Richmond to former fiancée, Sarah Elmira Royster Shelton, now a wealthy widow.

October 7, 1849 Dies mysteriously in Baltimore en route to Fordham to pursue editing job and prepare for his wedding.

Quotations and accounts of Poe's life are taken from the following sources. Those sources fully cited on page 63 are abbreviated here.

P. 4: "a wild weird clime ..." *The Complete Poetical Works of Edgar Allan Poe*, edited by John H. Ingram (*Poetical Works*), London and New York: Frederick Warne & Co., 1888, "Dreamland;" "'Literature is the most noble ..." P. 5: Ostrom (*Letters*), II: 427; P. 8: "They might hiss ..." Quinn, pp. 34-38; P. 10: "A nurse gave ..." Thomas and Jackson (*Poe Log*), p. 14; P. 10: "Unbeknownst to the three ..." *Poe Log*, p. 15; Pp. 10-11: "In this miserable ..." Quinn, Pp. 46-47; P. 11: "Asked about his background ..." Quinn, pp. 134-135 (Colonel James House letter, March 30, 1829); Pp. 11-12: "For my little son ..." *Poe Log*, pp. 3-4; Pp. 12 -13: "'From childhood's hour ...'" *Poetical Works*; P. 13: "a lovely little fellow ..." *Poe Log*, p. 18; P. 13: "When Edgar went to worship ..." Josh Gillespie, Director of Preservation Services, Historic Richmond Foundation, personal communication, May 2007; P. 14: "To a boy with an active imagination ..." Quinn, pp. 75-77; P. 14: "the first, purely ideal love ...'" *Letters*, II: 385 (October 1, 1848); P. 15: "'Helen, thy beauty ...'" *Poetical Works*; Pp. 16-17: "My determination is ..." *Letters*, I: 7; P. 18: "'[He] does nothing [for me] ..." *Poe Log*, p. 61 (November 1, 1824, letter); P. 18: "Poe was five foot eight ..." Deas., pp. 5, 7; P. 21: "'The Rhythmical Creation of Beauty'" Casuto (*Criticism*), p. 180 ("The Poetic Principle," by Edgar Allan Poe, *Sartrain's Union Magazine*, October 1850); P. 21: "I have thrown myself ...'" *Letters*, I: 10 (December 1, 1828); P. 24: "'It is evident that we ...'" Mabbott (*Collected Works*) II: 145; Pp. 25 to 26: "He wrote about murder ..." *The Deadly Truth: A History of Disease in America*, by Gerald N. Grob, Cambridge, MA: Harvard University Press, 2002, pp. 115-116; P. 26: "He wrote about disease ..." Grob, pp. 96-120; P. 26: "as the idea that individuals ..." *Murder Most Foul: The Killer and the American Gothic Imagination*, by Karen Halttunen, Cambridge, MA: Harvard University Press, 1998; P. 26: "'We tremble ...'" *Collected Works*, III: 1223; P. 27: "His salary: $10 a week ..." Ostrom, "Poe's Literary Labors and Rewards;" Pp. 27 to 29: "'My last my last my only ...'" *Letters*, I: 69 (August 29, 1835); P. 28: "'For Virginia ...'" *Letters*, I: 71 (August 29, 1835); P. 29: "'I have absolutely no pleasure ...'" Meyers, p. 89; Pp. 29 to 30: "[We] often find ourselves ...'" *Criticism*, p. 10 (*Southern Literary Messenger*, April 1836) P. 30: "We do not mean to say ..." *Criticism*, pp. 6-7 (*Southern Literary Messenger*, December 1835); P. 31: "the most discriminating ..." *Criticism*, p. 162; P. 31: "The greatest number ...'" *Poe Log*, p. 198 (William Leese Stone, *Commercial Advertiser*, April, 12, 1836); P. 32: "magazine prison house'" http://www.eapoe. org/works/essays/smprison.htm ("Some Secrets of the Magazine Prison House," by Edgar Allan Poe, *Broadway Journal*, February 15, 1845, 1: 103-104); P. 33: "'the death ... of a beautiful woman'" *Criticism*, p. 105 ("The Philosophy of Composition," *Graham's Magazine*, April 1846); P. 33: "authors wrote about beautiful women ..." Grob, p 109; P. 36: "I became insane ..." *Letters*, II: 356 (January 4, 1848); P. 36: "'namby pamby'" *Letters*, I: 197 (May 25, 1842); P. 37: "'unmerciful disaster ...'" *Poetical Works*; also *Letters*, II:372 (letter to Marie Louise Shew, June 1848); P. 37: "'Here comes Poe ...'" *Criticism*, p. 167 (*A Fable for the Critics*, by James Russell Lowell, New York: George P. Putnam, 1848); "'Deep into the darkness peering ...'" Pp. 38-39: *Poetical Works*; P. 40: "thoroughly unprincipled ...'" *Poe Log*, p. 648 ("Mr. English's Reply to Poe," by Thomas Dunn English, *The Morning Telegraph*, June 23, 1846); P. 41: "Love alone shall guide us ...'" Quinn, p. 499 (February 14, 1846, *Century Magazine* 1909 (79:893)); P. 42: "Shew paid for a coffin ..." *Poe Log*, pp. 669-685; P. 43: "'The skies they were ashen ...'" *Poetical Works*; P. 43: "Poe sold the poem ..." *Poe Log*, p. 707-708; P. 43: "We saw Mr. Poe ..." *Poe Log*, pp. 699-700; "'Deep in earth ...'" Pp. 44-45: *Bulletin of the New York Public Library*, December 1914 (18: 1462); "To the few who love me ..." P. 46: *The Works of Edgar Allan Poe*, by Edgar Allan Poe Tamerlane Edition (*Tamerlane Edition*), New York: The Judge Company, 1904, V: 5 (*Eureka: A Prose Poem*, by Edgar Allan Poe, New York: George P. Putnam, 1848); P. 47: "'All is life ...'" *Tamerlane Edition*, V: 155; P. 47: "Unless some true and tender ...'" *Letters*, II: 373; P. 47: "evidently committing a suicide ...'" Deas, p. 6; P. 48: "terrible impending doom'" *Poe Log*, p. 766 (Sarah Helen Whitman letter, October 25, 1875); P. 48: "'No person...,'" *Poe Log*, p. 767 (Whitman letter, March 20, 1874); P. 49: "wife of my soul" *Letters*, II: 401 (November 16, 1848); P. 49: "So long as I think ...'" *Ibid*; Pp. 49-50: "Think-oh *think* ...'" *Letters*, II: 402; P. 50: "The sickness-the nausea ...'" *Poetical Works*; Pp. 50-51: "But our love ...'" *Poetical Works*; P. 53: "Lord help my poor soul'" *Poe Log*, p. 846 (Dr. John J. Moran letter to Maria Clemm, November 15, 1849) ; "'I have been so ill ...'" Pp. 54-55: *Letters*, II: 452; "'The Poe character ...'" P. 56: *The Unknown Poe*, p. 91 (*Edgar Poe: His Life and Works*, by Charles Baudelaire, 1856); P. 57: "'Edgar Allan Poe is dead ...'" http://www.eapoe.org/PAPER/MISC1827/NYT49100.HTM ("Death of Edgar A. Poe, by "Ludwig," *The Daily Tribune*, October 9, 1849, p. 2); P. 59: "'And yet one cannot ...'" *Unknown Poe*, p. vii; Pp. 60-61: "In a dream ..." *Poe Poe Poe Poe Poe Poe Poe*, p. 29 (*Specimen Days*, by Walt Whitman, 1883).

RESOURCES

BOOKS

Deas, Michael J. *The Portraits and Daguerreotypes of Edgar Allan Poe.* Charlottesville, VA: University Press of Virginia, 1989.

Foye, Raymond (editor). *The Unknown Poe, an anthology of fugitive writings by Edgar Allan Poe, appreciations by Charles Baudelaire, Stephane Mallarme, Paul Valery, J.K.* Huysmans, & Andre Breton. San Francisco: City Lights Books, 1980.

Frank, Frederick S., and Anthony Magistrale. *The Poe Encyclopedia.* Westport, CT: Greenwood Press, 1997.

Hayes, Kevin J. (editor). *The Cambridge Companion to Edgar Allan Poe.* Cambridge: Cambridge University Press, 2002.

Hecker, William F. (editor). *Private Perry and Mister Poe: The West Point Poems, 1831, Facsimile Edition.* Baton Rouge, LA: Louisiana State University Press, 2005.

Hoffman, Daniel. *Poe Poe Poe Poe Poe Poe Poe.* New York: Doubleday, 1973.

Irwin, John T. *The Mystery to a Solution: Poe, Borges, and the Analytic Detective Story.* Baltimore, MD: The Johns Hopkins University Press, 1994.

Irwin, John T. *American Hieroglyphics: The Symbol of the Egyptian Hieroglyphics in the American Renaissance.* New Haven, CT: Yale University Press, 1980.

Kennedy, Gerald (editor). *A Historical Guide to Edgar Allan Poe.* Oxford: Oxford University Press, 2001.

Kennedy, J. Gerald, and Liliane Westerberg (editors). *Romancing the Shadow: Edgar Allan Poe and Race.* Oxford: Oxford University Press, 2001.

Meyers, Jeffrey. *Edgar Allan Poe: His Life and Legacy.* New York: Charles Scribner's Sons, 1992.

Poe, Edgar Allan. *Collected Works of Edgar Allan Poe.* Edited by Thomas Ollive Mabbott. Cambridge, MA: The Belknap Press of Harvard University Press, Volume I (Poems) 1969, Volumes II (Tales and Sketches 1831-1842) and III (Tales and Sketches 1843-1849) 1978.

Poe, Edgar Allan. *The Letters of Edgar Allan Poe.* Edited by John Ward Ostrom, Cambridge, MA: Harvard University Press, 1948.

Poe, Edgar Allan. *Edgar Allan Poe: Literary Theory and Criticism.* Edited by Leonard Cassuto. Mineola, NY: Dover Publications Inc., 1999.

Quinn, Arthur Hobson. *Edgar Allan Poe: A Critical Biography.* New York: Appleton-Century-Crofts, Inc., 1941.

Silverman, Kenneth. *Edgar A. Poe: Mournful and Never-ending Remembrance.* New York: Harper-Collins, 1992.

Silverman, Kenneth (editor). *New Essays on Poe's Major Tales.* Cambridge: Cambridge University Press, 1993.

Thomas, Dwight, and David K. Jackson. *The Poe Log: A Documentary Life of Edgar Allan Poe.* Boston, MA: G.K. Hall & Company, 1987.

Whalen, Terence. *Edgar Allan Poe and the Masses: The Political Economy of Literature in Antebellum America.* Princeton, NJ: Princeton University Press, 1999.

ARTICLES

Ostrom, John Ward. *"Poe's Literary Labors and Rewards, Myth and Reality."* The Edgar Allan Poe Society of Baltimore, 1983 lectures, copyright 1987/1998.

Kostyal, Arthur. "The Usual Suspect: Edgar Allan Poe, Consulting Detective." *Harper's Magazine*: January 2007, pp. 83-88.

WEB SITES/PLACES TO VISIT

The Poe Museum
1914 E. Main St.
Richmond, VA 23223
(888) 21E-APOE
www.poemuseum.org

Poe Society, Baltimore
www.eapoe.org

The Baltimore Poe House and Museum
203 Amity St.
Baltimore, MD
(410) 396-7932
http://www.eapoe.org/balt/poehse.htm

Edgar Allan Poe National Historic Site
532 N. Seventh St.
Philadelphia, PA
(215) 597-8780
http://www.nps.gov/edal/

Fordham Cottage
Knightsbridge Road and the Grand Concourse
The Bronx, NY
(718) 881-8900
http://www.bronxhistoricalsociety.org/
(click on Historic Houses)

The Raven Society (Poe at the University of Virginia)
www.uvaravensociety.com (click on Poe Resources)

***Knowing Poe*: Maryland Public Television**
http://knowingpoe.thinkport.org/default_flash.asp

***The Poe Shadow*, by Matthew Pearl**
(a novelist's take on Poe's death)
http://www.matthewpearl.com/poe/poe.html

INDEX

ILLUSTRATIONS CREDITS

Founded in 1888, the National Geographic Society is one of the largest nonprofit scientific and educational organizations in the world. It reaches more than 285 million people worldwide each month through its official journal, National Geographic, and its four other magazines; the National Geographic Channel; television documentaries; radio programs; films; books; videos and DVDs; maps; and interactive media. National Geographic has funded more than 8,000 scientific research projects and supports an education program combating geographic illiteracy.

For more information, please call 1-800-NGS LINE (647-5463) or write to the following address:
National Geographic Society, 1145 17th Street N.W. Washington, D.C. 20036-4688 U.S.A.

Visit us online at www.nationalgeographic.com/books. Librarians and teachers, visit us at www.ngchildrensbooks.org. Kids and parents, visit us at kids.nationalgeographic.com. For information about special discounts for bulk purchases, please contact National Geographic Books Special Sales: ngspecsales@ngs.org.For rights or permissions inquiries, please contact National Geographic Books Subsidiary Rights: ngbookrights@ngs.org.

Printed in U.S.A.